discovermore

Earth's Biomes

A Look at Deserts

Dwayne Hicks

Britannica Educational Publishing

IN ASSOCIATION WITH

THE ROSEN PUBLISHING GROUP

Published in 2027 by Britannica Educational Publishing (a trademark of Encyclopædia Britannica, Inc.) in association with The Rosen Publishing Group, Inc.
2544 Clinton Street, Buffalo, NY 14224

Distributed exclusively by Rosen Publishing.
To see additional Britannica Educational Publishing titles, go to rosenpublishing.com.

Editor: Greg Roza
Book Design: Michael Flynn

Photo Credits: Cover S.Borisov/Shutterstock.com; (series background) Dai Yim/Shutterstock.com; p. 4 Designua/Shutterstock.com; p. 5 Thasneem/Shutterstock.com; p. 6 schristinephoto/Shutterstock.com; p. 7 Delbars/Shutterstock.com; p. 9 (top) ABCDstock/Shutterstock.com; p. 9 (bottom) Marko Rupena/Shutterstock.com; p. 10 river34/Shutterstock.com; p. 11 Jiaye Liu/Shutterstock.com; p. 12 wild pro/Shutterstock.com; p. 13 Robert Stolting/Shutterstock.com; p. 14 Tavarius/Shutterstock.com; p. 15 Dimitrios Karamitros/Shutterstock.com; p. 16 arkanto/Shutterstock.com; p. 17 Loredana Habermann/Shutterstock.com; p. 18 Vladislav T. Jirousek/Shutterstock.com; p. 19 reisegraf.ch/Shutterstock.com; p. 21 (top) Joe Belanger/Shutterstock.com; p. 21 (bottom) abriendomundo/Shutterstock.com; p. 22 rontav/Shutterstock.com; p. 23 FotoRequest/Shutterstock.com; p. 24 Roberto Dani/Shutterstock.com; p. 25 Sean R. Stubben/Shutterstock.com; p. 26 Catay/Shutterstock.com; p. 27 karimjarmouni/Shutterstock.com; p. 28 M101Studio/Shutterstock.com; p. 29 DVY714/Shutterstock.com.

Cataloging-in-Publication Data

Names: Hicks, Dwayne.
Title: A look at deserts / Dwayne Hicks.
Description: New York : Britannica Educational Publishing, in association with Rosen Educational Services, 2027. | Series: Discover more: Earth's biomes | Includes glossary and index.
Identifiers: ISBN 9781641906265 (library bound) | ISBN 9781641906258 (pbk) | ISBN 9781641906272 (ebook)
Subjects: LCSH: Desert ecology--Juvenile literature. | Biotic communities--Juvenile literature.
Classification: LCC QH541.5.D4 H68 2027 | DDC 577.54--dc23

Manufactured in the United States of America

CPSIA Compliance Information: Batch #CSBRIT27. For further information contact Rosen Publishing at 1-800-237-9932.

Contents

What Is a Desert?

A desert is one type of biome. A biome is a large region of Earth that has a certain climate and certain types of living things. Some other biomes include tundra, forests, and grasslands.

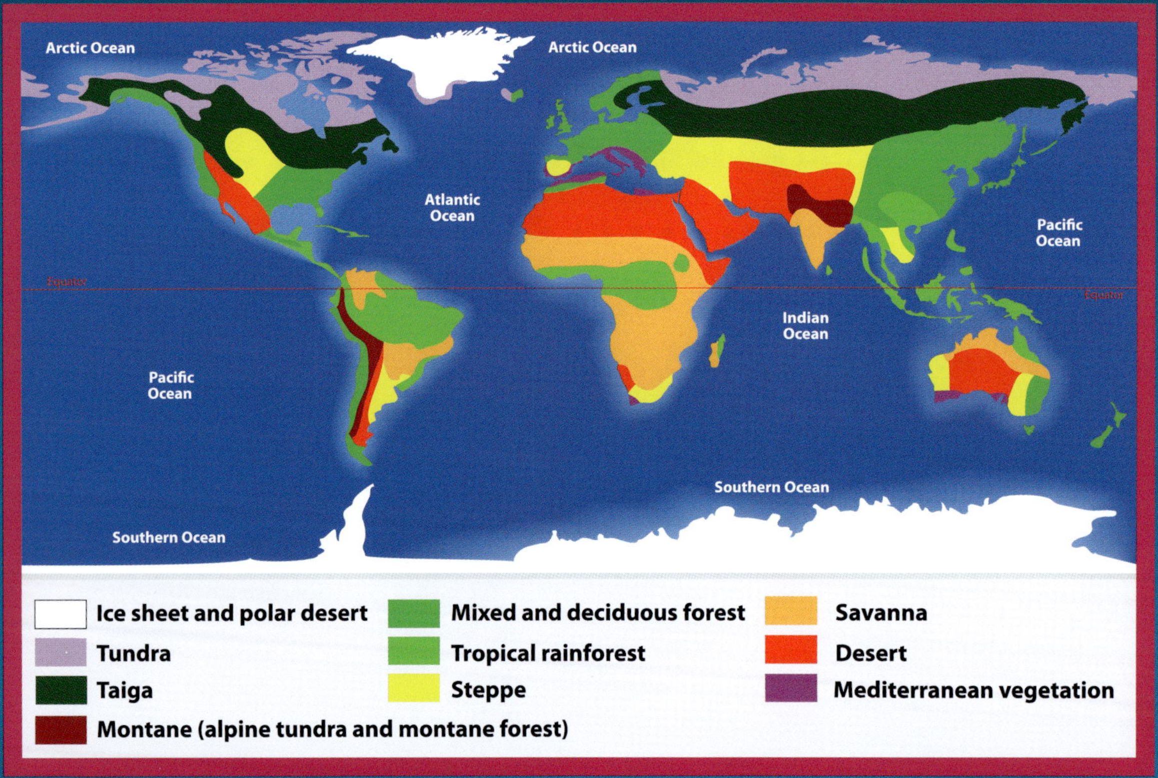

This map shows Earth's major biomes.

Many people think of camels when they think of desert animals.

When people think of a desert, they usually think of a sandy, hot, and dry place. But there are other types of deserts as well There are hot, cold, and temperate deserts.

A desert is any large region that gets very little rain each year. This lack of water means that very few plants or animals live in desert areas. The plants and animals that live in deserts around the world have traits that help them to survive in their particular areas. Deserts cover about 20 percent of Earth's land surface, and every continent has at least one desert.

Consider This

Camels can go many days without drinking water. Can you think of any other traits that would help animals live in a desert?

Yikes! That's Hot!

The world's hottest deserts are in areas closest to the **equator**, in the region known as the tropics. This is a band of Earth on either side of the equator. The sunlight is very strong in the tropics, which makes the area warmer than other parts of Earth.

The world's largest hot desert is the Sahara in northern Africa. Other hot deserts include the Mojave in the southwestern United States and the Kalahari in southern Africa.

Death Valley is a national park in California. The highest temperatures in the United States can be found there in summer.

The hottest location in the world might be in the Lut Desert of Iran. Weather satellites have recorded a high temperature of 177.4°F (80.8°C). Without weather stations on the ground, some scientists say they can't be sure it's the hottest place in the world.

In hot deserts daytime temperatures are often above 100° Fahrenheit (38° Celsius) in summer. Temperatures in Death Valley, California, have reached 134°F (56.7°C). Other desert areas around the world have reported higher temperatures, but they haven't been confirmed.

WORD WISE

THE EQUATOR IS AN IMAGINARY CIRCLE AROUND EARTH. IT RUNS EAST AND WEST AND IT IS HALFWAY BETWEEN THE NORTH AND SOUTH POLES.

The temperatures can drop surprisingly low in a hot desert. The air cools quickly after sunset. This is because the desert's air and bare earth are both dry. There are no clouds to trap heat in. The lack of clouds also means that the ground gets very hot when the sun rises. In non-desert biomes, clouds reflect much of the sunlight.

The temperature of the soil surface can rise even higher than the air temperature. Soil surface temperatures as high as 172°F (78°C) have been recorded in the Sahara. Some hot deserts have huge temperature differences depending on time of day. The temperatures can be 40° F (21.4° C) hotter during the day than at night.

Little rain and constant heat from the sun causes desert ground to crack.

compare and contrast

How much rain does the area where you live typically get? How hot does it typically get? Compare and contrast the climate you're used to with that of a hot desert.

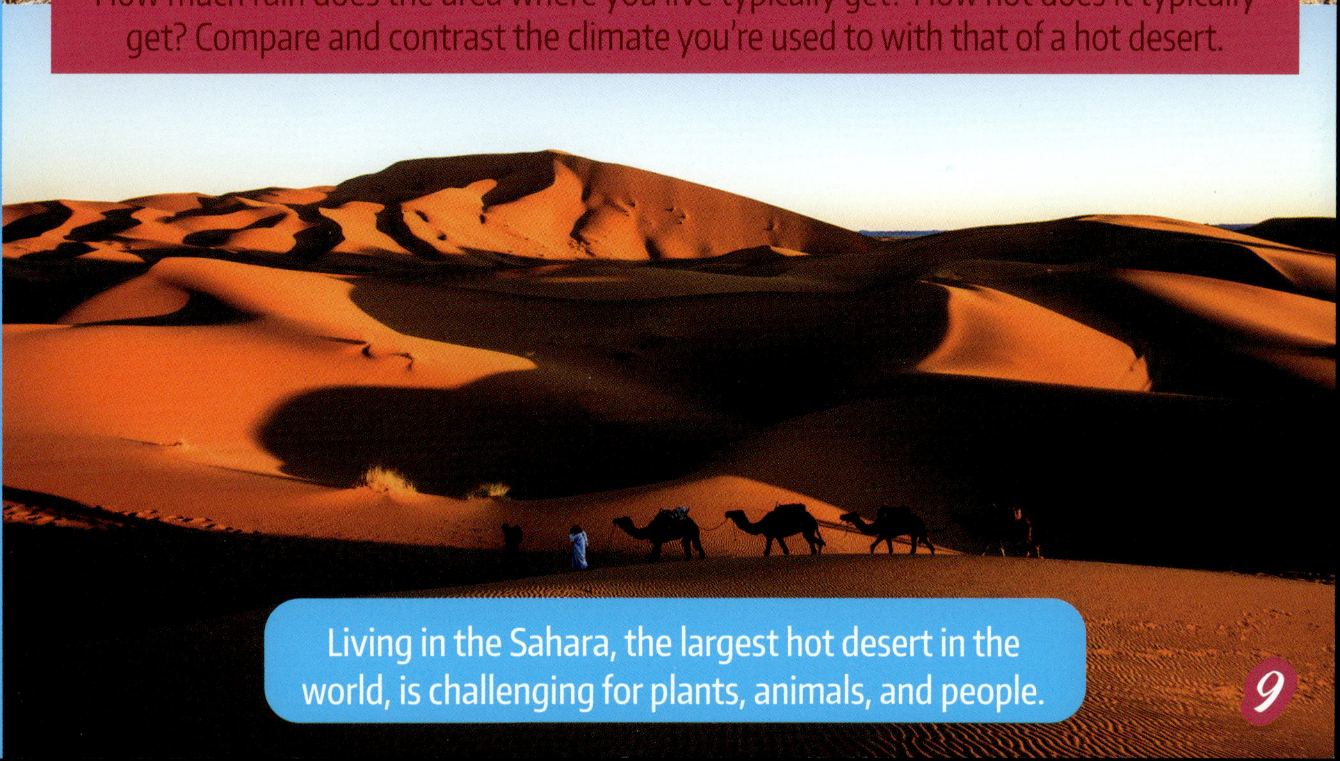

Living in the Sahara, the largest hot desert in the world, is challenging for plants, animals, and people.

Cold and Temperate Deserts

The two largest deserts on Earth are the Antarctic Desert and the Arctic Desert. These icy areas are cold deserts. Few things live there due to the freezing temperatures. Like all deserts, they get very little precipitation.

Antarctica is sometimes called the White Desert. Some areas receive only about 2 inches (5 cm) of precipitation a year.

A train crosses a vast plateau of the Gobi Desert in China. The Gobi is the largest temperate desert in the world.

Temperate deserts are found between the polar regions and the tropics, in the middle latitudes. They occur mainly in Central Asia. There are also smaller areas in western North America, southeastern South America, and Australia. These deserts are often separated from the coast by mountains or by great distance. Many temperate deserts exist in places high above sea level. This includes places between mountain ranges, called **plateaus**. Air picks up moisture from the ocean, but by the time it reaches these regions, it has lost much of it.

WORD WISE

PLATEAUS ARE RAISED, HIGH, FLAT AREAS, OFTEN SURROUNDED ON ONE OR MORE SIDES BY MOUNTAINS, CLIFFS, OR STEEP SLOPES.

The precipitation in a temperate desert can be in the form of rain or snow. Temperate deserts get most of their precipitation during the colder months. They have hot summers and cold winters.

Parts of the Gobi Desert in Mongolia receive snowfall in the winter.

Some areas of the Great Basin are more like a cold desert.

The biggest temperate desert is the Gobi in Central Asia. The biggest temperate desert in the United States is the Great Basin Desert, which covers nearly all of Nevada, western Utah, and portions of surrounding states. It includes the Great Sandy Desert of southeastern Oregon, the Snake River Plains of southern Idaho, the volcanic Black Rock Desert of northwestern Nevada, and the Great Salt Lake Desert of western Utah.

Consider This

When deserts do get precipitation, it can be a lot all at once. How do you think this affects the land, plants, and animals in a desert?

Along the Coast

Coastal deserts form near the shorelines of some landmasses. Most lie on the western coasts of South America and Africa. The winds in these areas tend to blow in such ways that they keep clouds with rain away from the land. Cold ocean currents also keep the air dry.

Water in coastal deserts comes mostly in the form of fog. Fog forms over the nearby oceans and then drifts over the deserts. Some water droplets condense on the leaves of plants, or even on the rocks or soil. The parts of coastal deserts that are closest to the water are warm but not hot during the summers and cool in winter. Further inland the deserts may be hotter.

The Namib Desert in southwestern Africa, shown here, is one example of a coastal desert.

compare and contrast

Name some ways that coastal deserts are similar to hot deserts. Now name some ways they are different.

The Atacama Desert stretches about 1,000 miles (1,600 km) along the western coast of South America.

Desert Shapes

Land features in deserts include dunes of shifting sand, mountains, bare rock, or plains of gravel and boulders. Sand dunes are not as common in deserts as many people think. For example, they make up only about 10 percent of the Sahara of northern Africa.

A common type of desert consists of mountains separated by basins called bolsons. The mountains receive most of the rains in downpours. As the water rushes down the steep slopes it cuts deep gullies.

This enormous sand dune in Morocco is named Erg Chebbi. "Erg" comes from the Arabic word for "dune field."

The Salar de Uyuni in Bolivia is the largest playa lake in the world.

Sometimes floodwaters make temporary shallow lake in basins. The lakes that form in basins with no outlet are called playa lakes. Typically the water **evaporates** or drains away, leaving behind sediments. The flat, sunken area left behind is called a playa.

WORD WISE

WATER EVAPORATES WHEN IT IS WARMED BY HEAT. HEAT CAUSES IT TO CHANGE FROM A LIQUID STATE (REGULAR WATER) TO A GAS THAT BECOMES PART OF THE AIR, KNOWN AS WATER VAPOR.

Plants of the Desert

Different desert plants have different ways of surviving in a dry climate. Some depend upon underground water and have long root systems or taproots that reach deep underground. Other plants can absorb water droplets in the air.

Welwitschia mirabilis grows only in the Namib Desert. This unique plant can grow a taproot up to 30 feet (9 m) long to reach underground water.

Pachycereus pringlei, more commonly called elephant cactus, is the largest cactus in the world. They are native to the Sonoran Desert of northern Mexico. The tallest elephant cactus on record grew to 63 feet (19.2 m) tall.

Ordinary non-desert plants take up water from the soil by means of their roots and give off water through their leaves. This process is called transpiration. Some desert plants, such as the cactus, have no leaves or only very small ones that usually drop off as the plant matures. They thus avoid a huge loss of water.

Cacti are succulent plants. This means that they have thick tissues that take up and hold large amounts of water. Cacti are able to withstand long dry periods by living on the stored water.

Consider This

Why do you think some desert plants grow only in one part of the world?

The yucca plant is another succulent that lives in deserts. They are members of the agave plant family that grows in North America. Yuccas store water in their thick, waxy leaves.

Some plants live in balance with their neighbors by growing quite far apart. This way, there is more water to go around. Trees and large shrubs can be found in some deserts, but there are not many of them in the driest ones.

Some desert plants survive by having unusual life cycles. Certain plants sprout when the rain falls, bloom quickly, ripen their seed in a few days, and then wither and die. Others survive a lack of water by drying up, just for a time. When water comes back, they go back to normal.

The largest yucca plant is the Joshua tree. They grow mainly in the Mohave Desert of the southwest United States.

compareandcontrast

How are yuccas and cacti similar, and how are they different?

Every five to seven years, wildflowers bloom in the Atacama Desert, despite it being the driest place on Earth. This turns the landscape pink for a short time.

Animals of the Desert

Desert animals have special characteristics, or traits, that help them survive in their surroundings. They have developed these traits through a process called **adaptation**. Animals live in all but the toughest desert environments.

Camels are very well adapted to living in deserts. In the Middle East, they are used similar to the way horses are used in the United States.

Burrowing owls, which are native to North America, use the abandoned underground homes of other desert animals for shelter.

For example, camels have adapted over many thousands of years to be able to go for long periods of time without drinking water. Most desert animals, including birds and insects, get the majority of their water from their food.

To save water and energy, animals might not move around much when it is hot or when water is low. They may hide from the sun during the hottest hours of the day and come out at night to feed. More than half of desert animals live at least part of the time underground, where it is cooler. Desert birds such as owls move to areas where it recently rained.

WORD WISE

ADAPTATION IS THE PROCESS BY WHICH SPECIES CHANGE OVER TIME TO BETTER SURVIVE WHERE THEY LIVE.

Australia's deserts have many kinds of reptiles that are not found anywhere else. Other kinds of animals, such as kangaroos, live there, too.

In the hot deserts of Africa and Asia, many of the larger animals are domesticated. Domestic animals are ones that have been tamed for use by humans. These include camels, donkeys, goats, sheep, and horses. Wild species such as gazelles, ibexes, and oryxes are rarer. Smaller animals, including rodents that burrow into the ground and reptiles like snakes and lizards, are more common.

The thorny devil lizard is native to the Australian Outback, a vast, dry area in the interior of the country. The lizard's thorns are an adaptation that guides water on its body to it's mouth.

Hadrurus arizonensis, or the giant hairy scorpion, lives in the Sonoran and Mojave Deserts. They feed on insects, spiders, rodents, lizards, and snakes.

Insects and spiders are common in deserts everywhere. Spiders, beetles, centipedes, moths, butterflies, ants, dragonflies and other bugs feed off plants and other small creatures. Insects and spiders provide a consistent source of food and water for larger animals.

Consider This

What is an advantage of being a smaller creature in the desert when it comes to getting food and water?

Desert People

Groups of people who traditionally live in the desert include the Tuareg of the Sahara, the San of the Kalahari, the Bedouins of the Middle East and North Africa, and the Aboriginal peoples of Australia. These groups have traditional practices to help them survive in the desert.

Many Tuareg people live in tents made of animal skins or rugs.

Tafilalt is the largest oasis in the Sahara. It's located in western Morocco.

Many desert dwellers live in oases. An oasis is a place in the desert with a supply of fresh water. A small number of Bedouin are **nomads**, who migrate into the desert during the rainy season. They move back to other areas in the drier seasons. They also dig wells, grow their own food, and raise animals such as sheep and goats.

In places that are too dry to grow crops, many peoples bring in water from nearby, wetter areas. This is a practice called irrigation. In North African and Asian oases and irrigated areas, some major foods grown include dates, figs, wheat, barley, rice, and beans.

WORD WISE

NOMADS ARE PEOPLE WHO HAVE NO PERMANENT HOME. THEY MOVE FROM PLACE TO PLACE TO FIND FOOD AND WATER FOR THEMSELVES AND THEIR ANIMALS.

Humans have changed deserts through the process of irrigation and through building projects. Some oases once only reached by camel now have airports and gas stations. Some deserts have valuable fossil fuels and minerals that people take out of the ground.

The desert has a balance of life that is easily broken. Too many new things, including new people moving there, can upset that balance.

Dubai was once a small, coastal fishing town in the United Arab Emirates. Today, it's one of the world's newest and largest cities!

To combat desertification near the Thar Desert in India, people have planted rows of jojoba plants to block the wind and swirling sand.

In other cases the actions of people have turned productive land into new deserts. This process is called desertification. It happens when people use the land too much for crops or get rid of too many trees in an area. Domesticated animals that humans raise for food can also destroy grasslands and other biomes, causing desertification. It also happens because of climate change.

Consider This

How do you think the growing human population will affect Earth's deserts ten or twenty years from now?

Glossary

burrow To dig a hole in the ground for shelter or protection. Also the hole itself.

climate change Changes to the world's climates over time, including changes in temperatures, precipitation, and wind patterns.

condense When matter changes from gas into a liquid.

date A fruit that grows on palms in some deserts.

fossil fuels Fuels, such as coal, oil, or natural gas, that formed in the earth from plant or animal remains.

gazelle A small, graceful swift antelope of Africa and Asia.

ibex A type of wild goat.

latitudes Areas of Earth measured by lines of latitude, or imaginary lines that circle Earth parallel to the equator.

oryx Any of several long-horned African antelopes.

precipitation Water that falls to the earth from clouds, in the form of rain, snow, sleet, mist, or hail.

satellite A spacecraft placed in orbit around Earth, a moon, or a planet to collect information or for communication.

sediment Matter that is left behind by water, wind, or glaciers.

shrub a woody plant that has several stems and is smaller than most trees.

species A particular type of living thing.

taproot A large main root that grows straight down and gives off many smaller side roots.

tundra A treeless plain in the Arctic regions of the world.

For More Information

Books

Doty, Abby. *Death Valley*. Mendota Heights, MN: Focus Readers, 2026.

Eason, Sarah. *Deserts*. Shrewsbury, UK: Cheriton Children's Books, 2026.

Websites

How Desert Animals Thrive in the Hottest Regions of the World
animals.howstuffworks.com/animal-facts/desert-animals.htm
Read more about unique adaptations for desert animals from all over the word.

Tuareg People Facts for Kids
kids.kiddle.co/Tuareg_people
Learn all about the Tuareg people of the Sahara.

Index